Who Is Warren Buffett?

The Staircase He Took to Success

The Story of a Man Whose Investment Strategies Made Him a World Famous Billionaire But Whose Wisdom Made Him a Legend

By Phil Cooper

"The most important investment you can make is in yourself."

— Warren Buffett

Who Is Warren Buffett?

When life gives you lemons, you make lemonade. You can then sell that lemonade to make money that you can use to buy more lemons. Warren Buffett's story is similar to this situation because he used every resource and turned it into another step on the staircase to success.

Warren had a passion for reading and a penchant for numbers since his childhood. Even as a child, he realized he had a gift and used it to start businesses and ventures from an early age. His first investment in stocks at the age of 11 is proof of him knowing his potential. From that age to now, being a 91-year-old billionaire, the man's name still gets around.

This book will take you on a ride to Warren Buffett's life, where you will likely experience more uphill than downhill. Let the advice of the CEO of Berkshire Hathaway Inc. compiled in this e-book guide you on how to invest in not a business but your future. Learn how you can adopt his talent to find a good investment and become sustainably wealthy.

Table of Contents

Introduction

In today's age of the internet and social media, people have become more financially literate than ever in today's technology-driven times than ever. But what made an eleven-year-old invest in stocks before the age of technology?

The infamous holding company Berkshire Hathaway Inc. CEO Warren Buffett is among the most well-known billionaires. You'd see many people leaving or entering the list of wealthiest people on the planet year after year. However, you'll see Warren Buffett's name being a fixture on that list.

Warren Buffett's love for reading and his eye for good investments have brought him among the world's wealthiest people. The man has had an aptitude for numbers since he was a child. He had developed a great understanding of compounding and how to make money work for you in the age when other kids were busy playing games.

Nicknamed the Oracle of Omaha, the Nebraska-born man is not just famous because of his wealth over the years. He is a man who believes in giving back. And that's what he aims to do with his knowledge and wealth.

Buffett has pledged to give away 99% of his wealth to charities, including the Bill and Melinda Gates Foundation. He also invited other billionaires to contribute to this noble cause. And so, billionaires like Bill Gates, Elon Musk, and Mark Zuckerberg said 'aye, aye' to that, pledging to give away 50% of their wealth for noble causes.

The man has also generously distributed his knowledge by giving financial advice on numerous forums and talk shows. He's well known for introducing and propagating the idea of passive income. He's a firm believer in investing in businesses and start-ups whose objectives are well-fitting with his ideologies.

Despite being a billionaire, you'd find Buffett's frugal way of living most appealing. Buying meals from McDonald's to save the costs of food and living in the same house in Omaha that he bought in 1958 are some of the things that make him relatable and approachable. These personal quirks also set him apart from other billionaires. Perhaps, due to this reason, people hold onto his every word because a man from such a humble background created an empire but lived just like the non-wealthy population.

Warren Buffett is also known for his views on malpractice on Wall Street. He believes that businesses should conduct themselves fairly and ethically. Buffett has also been outspoken about the issue of the rich paying fewer taxes. Despite all of it, he's often criticized for the monopoly he has created and sold to people.

Whether you love him or hate him, you can agree that we all have much to learn from this man. Whether it's how to run a business, invest wisely, or just the general way of living life, Buffett has something to offer everyone. Use this book to guide you in making wise decisions when dealing with your wealth and paving your own path to success.

The Story of Warren Buffett

"After 25 years of buying and supervising a great variety of businesses, Charlie [Munger] and I have not learned how to solve difficult business problems. What we have learned is to avoid them."

Some people believe passion is more important than innate talent. Others believe that natural abilities beat passion. Debating the importance of passion over ability has been going on forever. However, Warren Buffett is the perfect example of the very few who can balance both.

The Berkshire Hathaway Inc. CEO has been gifted with extraordinary computational skills and a passion for learning something new and constantly challenging himself. Many have often referred to him as a mathematical prodigy of his time. But if talent were all, would his ventures have been sustainably successful?

Born on August 30th, 1930, Warren Edward Buffett was the son of a stockbroker and future congressman, Howard Buffett. His mother, Leila Buffett, was a homemaker. He was a middle child with two sisters. The family lived in Omaha, Nebraska, and was trying to survive during the times of the world's biggest market crash, The Great Depression.

Howard, a stockbroker with Union State Bank who had just joined the business two years before the crash, was in distress. He had a family to take care of but had no means to do so. However, just about a few weeks after Warren's first birthday, two of Howard's partners brought a new opportunity to him: Buffett, Sklenicka & Co., a stock brokerage firm.

While the government's poor decisions pulled numerous banks and businesses deep into the whirlwind of financial panic, Buffett's company was doing good. Within a couple of years, despite facing health issues, Howard Buffett was able to give his family a life of financial stability with Buffett & Co.

However, all was not rosy. Not many people know that young Warren and his older sister Doris faced verbal abuse from his mother. The Buffett household had no tradition of saying "I love you." While the elder Buffet provided a sense of security, he could not protect his children from Leila's lashes. Leila never let her rage out in front of her husband and often blamed neuralgia as the cause of all her temper. By the time Warren was three, his mother's bitterness had been stamped on his heart.

In contrast, his mother had a loving attitude toward his younger sister Roberta. Young Warren sought warmth and refuge in his aunt Alice. Aunt Alice was Howard's unmarried sister, who gave extra attention to Warren. She was the one who motivated Warren to seek new adventures and aided him in exploring his new interests.

As an introvert, Warren would spend hours thinking about numbers. He was fascinated by time and the art of calculating odds. He'd grab his newly gifted stopwatch, courtesy of his favorite aunt, and race marbles in the bathtub for hours. After the sermons, he'd calculate the life span of hymn composers.

At the tender age of 6, he had understood that numbers were everywhere around him. To calculate odds, he had to find as much information as possible. Young Warren had an unstoppable passion and an eye for seeing probabilities everywhere. These qualities paved the way for Warren to become an entrepreneur early in his life.

Warren's love for reading, solving mysteries, and collecting data made him even more unique as a child. He collected number plate data with his kindergarten friend to have information if someone committed a robbery at a nearby bank. He had also become sharp-minded with his newfound interest in playing bridge; he still plays with his best friend and fellow billionaire Bill Gates.

His Early Successful Ventures

"Money is not everything. Make sure you earn a lot before speaking such nonsense."

Warren started to seek out new ways of making money from the age of six. Early on, it was a game for him, one that he understood and loved playing. He had tried numerous ways to do so.

Door-to-Door Selling

Young Buffett started going door-to-door to sell stuff. He began by selling packs of chewing gum. He'd buy gum from his paternal grandfather's grocery shop and then sell it at a profit. He sold each pack for a nickel and never sold the pieces separately, one of the values that he'd set for himself.

Warren then started selling Saturday Evening Post and Liberty magazines door to door. He began wearing a money changer on his belt that made him feel professional. It also satiated his desire for collecting; he was now collecting cash.

Having a knack for knowing which business or venture is in demand and would generate more profit, Warren set out to sell Coca-Cola cans in the summer. He'd go to the beach and sell thirsty visitors chilled, satisfying soda pop. He soon started to become more interested in the game and, this time, in making money.

At age nine, one of his crazy ideas got into trouble with the cops. He used to go around a nearby golf field, collect used golf balls around the course, and sell them to the players there. He was kicked out once he was caught.

Warren was selling peanuts and popcorn during football games at the University of Omaha by ten. His earnings were taken away once due to his political views against Franklin Delano Roosevelt. However, he learned that day to keep everything else aside when acquiring hard-earned money.

Buying His First Stock

Warren enjoyed hanging out at his father's office at the Omaha National Bank building. He'd read numerous books on his father's bookshelf, learning more about numbers and business. Two floors down his father's office, the stock prices were marked on a chalkboard.

Warren would visit this place with his maternal great Uncle John Barber and paternal great Uncle Frank Buffett. Both older gentlemen weren't fond of each other but tried to predict the share prices and convince Warren to get on their side. Warren loved spending time with them, but he didn't understand the numbers on the electronic display.

It was the first time Warren was finding something difficult to grasp. He was sure that both his uncles weren't talking much sense when predicting the stock prices. Warren was smart enough to know that wherever there are numbers, there ought to be a pattern. He just couldn't comprehend the pattern of fluctuating stock prices.

Papa Buffett took young Buffett on an East Coast trip at age ten. It was a tradition in the household that you could choose the places you wanted to visit on the East Coast at ten. Any other kid would have chosen the fanciest amusement park; Warren wished to visit the New York Stock Exchange, Scott Stamp and Coin Company, and Lionel Train Company.

Howard Buffett took his son to the largest brokerage firm Goldman Sachs, and both got to meet the famous Sidney Weinberg. The two adults talked for half an hour while young Warren listened earnestly. The visit to Weinberg's well-furnished office made Warren realize that he was in the presence of an important man.

After the meeting, they went on to the New York Stock Exchange. Awestruck, Warren watched the hustle-bustle of the place, having a surreal experience. Then, he observed a man rolling a cigar for someone, and the idea of wealth and abundance made him promise to himself that he too would become a millionaire by the age of 35.

He knew he had a lot of money to accumulate to achieve his goal. One fateful day, he got his hands on the book One Thousand Ways to Make $1,000 at the Benson library. He eagerly read all the knowledge from the book that contained precise and practical advice to achieve what the book's title said.

The idea that got him the most cash for his first stock came from the same book: buying a pennyweight machine. He understood compounding well, and his brain started to compute like a machine. He went on to invest in the pennyweight machine and earned profits.

The earnings from the pennyweight machine and his previous ventures went into purchasing his first stock. At age 11, he bought three shares of Cities Service Preferred at $114.75. Doris, his elder sister, was his partner in these purchases.

The market hit a low in a few months, and the stock price went from $38 to $27. Doris constantly reminded him of the decreasing prices, making him afraid of losing money and somewhat responsible. So, when the price plummeted to $40 each, he sold the shares, happy with the profit he had earned.

Young Warren's first few self-learned financial lessons took place when the prices of the shares skyrocketed and reached $202 each share. Disappointed with his decision, he swore never to rush to get small returns nor constantly worried about the price he had paid and never took responsibility for somebody else's money. The lessons he learned that day guided him into making informed choices today.

Newspaper Selling and Farming Business

When Warren was about ten, he helped his father
in his election campaign. Seeing FDR run for another term,
Howard had decided to stand up in the elections for
Nebraska. Although Nebraska was a Democrat state,
Howard stood as a Republican and somehow managed to
win against his somewhat overconfident opponent.

Soon the family moved to Virginia while Howard
rented an apartment in Washington DC for work. Every
member of the Buffett family had a different experience
and reaction to the move. While others in the family
seemed well adjusted, Warren succeeded in making his
paternal grandfather believe that he wasn't doing well in
DC and was soon on a train back to Omaha.

After school, Warren was back in his old
neighborhood and worked at his grandfather's grocery
shop. The trivial manual tasks his grandfather gave him
made him realize that manual labor wasn't for him. Once
shoveling away the heavy snow with his friend, Warren
and his companion only got a total of 20 cents in payment

from his grandfather. The experience taught him to know his deals before taking up a task.

Warren's changing attitude due to the freedom and autonomy he got at Omaha worried his parents. They decided to take him back with them to Washington. Warren suffered miserably at school there because his attitude and personality were no longer of the sweet boy who loved to please everyone.

Instead of focusing on his grades, Warren decided to deliver newspapers to earn cash. He took on two newspapers in the morning, the Washington Post and the Times-Herald, and one in the afternoon, the Evening Star. Soon, he left his two morning papers for delivering the Westchester only to selected houses.

While delivering the papers, Warren also collected scrap newspapers and magazines that he sold according to weight for a few cents in return. He also collected data to identify the expiring magazine subscriptions and found another job for himself. He now started selling and renewing magazine subscriptions door-to-door.

The job of selling magazines and newspapers had earned him so well that he had made his first thousand in savings in no time. At the age of 14, Warren Buffett had filed his first tax return and paid $7, cutting the cost of his watch and bicycle as business investments.

At 15 years of age, having passed his tenth grade from Woodrow Wilson High School, Warren had a total savings of $2,000. He invested in his father's new venture with Carl Falk called Builders Supply Co. Young Buffett then went on to buy a tenant farm in Thurston County, Nebraska, for $1,200; he was now a businessman.

Pinball Machines and Other Small Businesses

Warren was always looking for new ways of making money. This interest in making money made him famous around Woodrow Wilson High. However, behind that smart, talented businessman facade was hiding a boy who was dealing with his own insecurities.

Ever since leaving Omaha, he felt a bit less gifted when it came to pleasing people. His genius would scare people away. Warren was ruthless in proving his smartness despite being shy and almost innocent. That often happened when people debated him.

He always managed to get on people's nerves during debates, even if he was wrong. His attitude contributed to keeping the debates going and adding more fun to them. However, it caused people to interact with him less and less. He knew he stood out from the crowd, but he wasn't among the favored ones of teachers and peers like in Omaha.

His grades also kept dropping miserably except for in typing. That, too, became a competition for him because by typing hastily and loudly, he agitated others and made them feel like they were going slow, so in trying to speed up, they would make errors. All these tactics of acting superior were only for making up for his feelings of inadequacy.

Perhaps he couldn't make friends because it didn't depend on numbers. Warren's mind had always understood numbers and only trusted them, disregarding abstract concepts that didn't make sense to him. He then stumbled upon Dale Carnegie's How to Win Friends and Influence People. Instead of believing the legend blindly, he started conducting a secret experiment to collect data.

Warren would interact with people, sometimes following Carnegie's advice and sometimes behaving like his old self. Some of the Carnegie's advice he followed were:

- Don't criticize. Appreciate.
- Call out people's names when talking to them; they love the attention.
- Instead of ordering someone to do a task, humbly ask them to do it. And so on.

He would observe how people responded to him when he sounded more like himself and how people responded when he talked gently, following the book's advice. He collected the data and was fascinated to find that the odds were proving that his methods worked in Carnegie's favor. So, time after time, he'd go back to the book, using it as a manual for making friends.

His slowly-changing nature got him into Woodrow Wilson's golf team and helped him get the first few skills needed to become a salesman. That's how he could establish three more businesses on the side: Buffett's Golf Balls, Buffett's Approval Service, and Wilson's Coin-Operated Machine Company.

Buffett's Golf Balls sold refurbished golf balls that Warren got from a seller from Chicago. Warren and his friend Don Danly sold a pack of dozen for six bucks, but their families never even came to know of their business or who they were dealing with. His golf team members thought Warren was going out collecting the balls from water traps himself.

Buffett's Approval Service sold sets of stamps to people mostly outside the state. Warren also started his own showroom with his friend Lou Battistone at Lou's father's used-car lot. He soon gave up that idea as car washing required manual labor, which was something Warren didn't enjoy, even for an extra amount of cash.

His most successful venture from the day was Wilson's Coin-Operated Machine Company. Warren and his friend Don Danley, who was in charge of operations, went on to buy pinball machines and set them up at barbershops. To experiment with whether it worked, they went to a nearby barbershop and asked the owner Mr. Erico for permission with half of the money they made, to which Mr. Erico agreed.

Warren bought a used pinball machine for twenty-five bucks and set it up at Mr. Erico's barbershop. Soon, the waiting customers at the barbershops started filling their time by playing pinball. On the first day, they earned four bucks, and all parties were pleased.

The idea became so popular that soon every barbershop in the nearby neighborhood too had a pinball machine that Warren bought with the sales from the previous one. His compounding skills were being polished while making him good money.

His salesmanship was also improving as he had to convince barbershop owners that maintaining pinball machines is expensive, so they don't go off buying a pinball on their own. Warren had also learned one of the most important lessons of capital through his pinball machine's success: money works for the owner, not vice versa.

While earning money from all the legal means, Warren had somehow succeeded in learning a few illegal methods of money-making. Thanks to the guys at Silent Sales, the shop where they bought their used pinball machines, Warren had some crooked ideas of his own cooking in his brain. Warren and Danly had somehow managed to create fake coins with the help of his coin collection and were using those coins for small purchases such as soda etc.

Teenage Buffett was making $175 a month, which was more than his own teachers during his high school days. By the time he finished high school, Warren had accumulated $5,000, most of which came from his newspaper business. Warren had now trained himself in using money to make more money and never stopped doing so.

Investing in Himself: His Biggest Accomplishment

"Imagine that you had a car, and that was the only car you'd have for your entire lifetime. Of course, you'd care for it well, changing the oil more frequently than necessary, driving carefully, etc. Now, consider that you only have one mind and one body. Prepare them for life, care for them. You can enhance your mind over time. A person's main asset is themselves, so preserve and enhance yourself."

Warren graduated sixteenth out of 350 students in his high school class. He spent that summer working as a relief circulation manager for Times-Herald.

After graduating high school, Warren went to study college at the University of Pennsylvania Wharton business school in 1947. Although he was not in favor of formal schooling, young Buffett could not refuse Papa Buffett's decision. Hence, his struggles at Penn began.

Warren was a smart kid but not emotionally mature. His prodigal mind assisted him in passing classes without putting in much effort. Still, he could never manage to make new friends at the University of Pennsylvania, where most of the students came to learn and enjoy the social scenes. Warren was socially awkward, and dating was one thing he kept failing at miserably.

He would sing around his dorm room, disturbing his roommate and a family acquaintance, Chuck. Warren knew that with his habits of being a sloppy teenager, nobody would keep up with him, but his immature social side of the brain didn't pay much heed to it. He continued being himself, hoping to get through the four school years with the same attitude.

In his classes, Warren was an absolute show-off. He would entertain some of his teachers by quoting their exact words back to them. He'd mostly be the first to finish during exams; he once completed his exam even before the teacher had completed passing the exam paper around.

Warren attended frat parties not to find dates but to hang out and find an audience to talk about stocks. He'd turn whoever he debated with on stocks to dust with his experience and knowledge. He took pride in that but was losing his abilities to charm people as he used to in Omaha.

Warren was getting tired at UPenn. He was also required to meet UPenn's physical education credits. While numerous sports were famous at the university and other students participated with zeal, Warren never enjoyed it.

For Warren, rowing as a sport worked in various ways: it required pattern and rhythm, just like ping pong, that he enjoyed. The only downside to rowing was that it was a team sport, and Warren was not a team player. The only team he loved being in was for his business because he could instruct and lead the operations instead of just playing a part.

Young Buffett was happy to return home for his summer vacations in Washington, where he continued his job as a relief circulation manager at Times-Herald. His sisters had gotten jobs and worked while Warren reconnected with his friend Don Danly and enjoyed the rest of his days there. Don's girlfriend set up Warren for the summer with her friend Bobbie, but Warren was back at the university as soon as the vacations were over.

Warren liked systems: he liked learning about them and following them. And so, the only two classes he genuinely enjoyed were Industry 101 by Professor Hockenberry and Business Law by Professor Cataldo. He admired the latter because of the photographic memory of his teacher and was excited to share his own prodigal brain's talents with the professor.

In 1948, Truman won the elections as the president, whereas Warren's father Howard lost Congress. The move from Washington back to Omaha gave Warren a perfect excuse to leave Penn. He decided to join the University of Nebraska in Lincoln: the latter being much cheaper than the former. Warren could relate to these his peers at his new college better.

Warren immediately started working a summer job at Lincoln Journal as country circulation manager upon returning to Nebraska. It was tough for him to manage rural boys and ensure their work was up to the mark. Warren realized the troubles and responsibilities that came with a managing job when he added a girl to the team. Some of the boys he hired quit saying he had made it a girl's job.

Neither his struggles at the University of Pennsylvania Wharton business school nor the challenges as a manager were as eye-opening for Warren as the Harvard Business School rejection.

Upon completing his graduation from the University of Nebraska, Warren decided to join Harvard Business School while juggling his small businesses and a sales job at JC Penney's. Though he was still against formal schooling, he was smart enough to know that Harvard was the only place to provide him prestige and a worthy network. He didn't even have to pay for the school: he had won a scholarship of five hundred dollars through a newspaper ad where only Warren showed up.

Warren didn't prepare himself much for his Harvard interview in Chicago. Though his grades weren't stellar, he was confident that the experienced professionals at Harvard would realize his innate talents and prodigal mind. If that had failed, Warren was convinced that his early life ventures and the knowledge about stocks, which convinced people of his genius, would make him noticeable.

Warren had miscalculated (something he normally doesn't do) about Harvard because they were looking for leadership qualities, not a salesman persona. So, from first sight, the Harvard interviewer saw Warren for his true immature self and not for the smart-aleck facade that he had managed to hide behind for years. This event left young Buffett confused because he was confident he'd win; Warren didn't know where he had gone wrong.

The pivotal episode only thrust Warren forward in the direction of his dreams. At times, it's not what we wish for but what we truly need that life really brings us.

Something similar happened for Warren, and things started falling in place together.

On an August morning, while casually flipping through the pages of the Columbia catalog, Warren came across a name that put the flipping to a halt. Benjamin Graham, the renowned author of one of the greatest books in the history of investment, The Intelligent Investor, was a faculty at Columbia. The man had written a systematic manual on getting into and succeeding in the investment world with such precision that anyone willing could easily understand stocks.

Warren had cherished the book as he loved to learn systems. The practical examples from the book helped Warren himself learn more about stocks despite his broad knowledge of the subject. The great author of the world-famous book was teaching finance at Columbia University.

Much to his surprise, he came across another maestro in investment, David Dodd, co-author of Security Analysis with Benjamin Graham and associate dean of the department of finance at the university. Security Analysis was the more analytical version of The Intelligent Investor and was written more than a decade before the latter. Warren sat there stunned, not believing his luck, but he knew he had to take a step soon.

Although admissions had closed at the University, Warren wrote a personalized letter to Dodd, who was also in charge of the admissions. David was touched by Warren's honesty. He wasn't fazed by Warren's immaturity. David instead saw the true passion in a kid who wanted to do big in this world and had the talent to do so. Surprisingly, Warren Buffet has stated that he doesn't remember the contents of this letter.

Though there was only a month left in the classes to start, David accepted Warren's sincere permission to come and study under the guidance of two legends in the world of investment. Columbia was the place that believed in teaching craft, unlike Harvard's leadership approach for admitting candidates. From that day on, there was no going back for Buffett, whose last name would be enough as an introduction in the years to come.

Becoming a Mentee Under Benjamin Graham and David Dodd

"The best thing I did was to choose the right heroes."

Once Warren reached New York City in the fall of 1950, he knew he was on his own. Howard Buffett was preparing for reelection to Congress, which meant his family might have to move back to Washington if he won. Warren was now in unfamiliar territory with no maternal attention from his aunt and no one to substitute for paternal support.

Despite his savings, earnings, and investments in stocks, Warren was frugal as ever. Due to his late admission, he could not get a dorm room and chose to stay at the YMCA, paying a dime a day. He knew and understood the truth behind the saying, "a penny saved is a penny earned."

David Dodd warmly welcomed Warren in his first session of the Finance Class Investment management and security analysis. Warren's prodigal mind had the textbook of the course Security Analysis etched on his memory. He was able to quote the book better than the author himself.

David's class, just like his book, contained not just the principles of a subject matter but practical examples too. David had written the famous book by sitting in Graham's seminar to collect his wisdom and use his own experience in the field of investment. His class now broadly discussed railroad bonds.

Warren got paternal affection and attention from David. David introduced Warren to his family and invited him several times for dinner. He also appreciated Warren's eagerness to learn instead of dismissing it as immaturity.

Warren had come across some of the best students and business minds in the country at Columbia. However, the interaction with these students still consisted of him trying to discuss and share his stock knowledge. On one such event, Warren was effortlessly rambling about stocks in his usual hyperactive style to convince Bob Dunn, the most intelligent guy in his class. In turn, Bob's flatmate

Fred Stanback became his student. Fred went on to invest in stocks for the first time the same day.

Warren was also convinced during those years that Marshall-Wells, a hardware store he and his father had jointly invested in, was going to get them a good return. With his professor's permission, Warren cut David's class one day and attended Marshall-Wells' annual meeting in Jersey City with Fred. That's where he came across Walter Schloss, one of the Graham-Newman Corporation's employees.

With a series of frauds and uneventful financial losses that Walter had faced during his life, he learned the value of wealth early. The family continued to persevere, though, and eventually, after many struggles and rejections, Walter managed to get a job at Graham-Newman. Walter had also been Graham's student in the same course that Warren was enrolled in.

In the same meeting, Warren came across another influential name in the world of investment, Louis Green. Green wasn't only an investor and Graham's ally. Together

Green, Graham, and Newman sought to buy a company's majority shares for the price of peanuts and drive the management and operations of the company by becoming a member of the board of directors.

He had hit a lottery that day and managed to play this golden ball in his favor. He conversed with Green and ended up having lunch with him alongside Stanback. At lunch, when Green inquired Warren about his interest in Marshall-Wells, instead of giving a well-reasoned answer, Warren ended up quoting it as Benjamin Graham's advice. Lou replied that he must start thinking for himself instead of following in other people's footsteps.

To avoid repeating the mistake in his class with Graham that was about to begin in a few weeks, Warren got himself educated on his educator as much as possible. In his search for a better understanding of the man, Warren had an hours-long conversation with Lorimer Davidson, the financial vice president of GEICO, Government Employees Insurance Company. Graham-Newman owned fifty-five percent of the company.

Warren was fascinated with how the operations at GEICO were managed. It was a company that provided auto insurance to government employees. Davidson, a man of resilience, started in the company by selling stocks and persevered to climb to the top to become its vice president.

Warren had always been fascinated with life expectancy. Therefore, an insurance company's work appealed to him. He quickly grasped the knowledge he got from Davidson and went on to cash three-fourths of his stock investments and buy GEICO shares.

Warren had made calculated projections of the share prices and overall value of GEICO over the next five years. However, Graham was against making projections. He was skeptical of using stock value to make projections and invest according to the economic crisis of 1929 that left a mark on his memory. He taught it the principle of using value stocks for making projections but never believed in applying it to his own company.

Graham, though a genius, was quite appalled by the idea of interacting with people much. He couldn't hold a conversation with fellow humans for more than a few minutes because he got bored. That was why, unlike Dodd, Graham wasn't wooed by Warren's prodigal mind or his accomplishments.

Graham had his own, as Warren later quoted, "protective coating" and that no one got to be intimate with him. Facing the ups and downs of business, he learned to play the investment game with risk-free strategies. Graham-Newman Corporation, owned by Benjamin Graham and Jerry Newman, is one of the few firms that beat the stock market with an average of 2.5% a year.

Graham used numerous examples and analogies to make concepts easily digestible for his students. His favorite activities included comparing two different companies, one performing well and the other underperforming, and analyzing the reasons. It turned out that both the companies under discussion were the same but at different times.

Graham's depiction of the stock's intrinsic value and people's conviction of the stock's value as Class 1 truth and Class 2 truth, respectively, had made him immensely popular. No matter what it may seem to the onlookers, Class 1 truth is the crucial factor. Graham's examples and other teaching methods aided Warren in understanding three of the most primary and imperative principles of investing:

Margin safety is essential. The boundary you set or the room you provide yourself for making errors, even in good investment decisions.

The fluctuation of stock prices in the market does not indicate the company's value and shouldn't influence your decisions.

A stock is a fraction of the part of the business that one can own.

The margin safety principle greatly influenced Warren as all the other things can be calculated, but margin safety is a risk: the only way not to lose is never to stop.

Apart from these basic principles, Warren also learned and understood what Graham meant when he wrote the article, "Is American Business Worth More Dead Than Alive?" for Forbes in 1932. Graham pointed out that you can best calculate a business's value by looking at its value if it's liquidated. Often dead companies are worth more than when they were alive and in business as liquidation can generate more interest and return per share than the business ever had when running.

Warren learned a great deal from his mentor, who was always ready to answer before anyone else. His classmates recall that the class seemed more like a duet and less like a seminar, thanks to Warren's eagerness to answer every question and ask new ones. Warren was the only one to pass Graham's class with an A+ grade.

Judging by his accomplishments in the class, Warren was confident that he would land a job at Graham-Newman. He had proved himself to be a stellar student throughout and researched and practiced the principles he learned beyond the classroom. After graduating in 1952, he knew what his next step would be.

To say Warren was shocked when Graham rejected him for a job at his firm is an understatement. He could feel Harvard's rejection scene repeating itself. This time, the only difference was that Graham only hired Jewish people at his company. He wasn't biased, just a man of his principles who wanted to give the marginalized population of that time a better chance in the world: hiring Buffett would have been a prejudice instead.

Warren returned to Omaha in spring and went on to serve in the National Guard. Though he wasn't well-suited to be a National Guard, his other option was serving in Korea. Warren chose the former option for obvious reasons.

After fulfilling his obligations to the country, Warren returned to and settled in Omaha, far from his family in Washington. Howard Buffett had been re-elected as Congressman. Once again, their life was a juggle between Washington and Omaha. Warren was pretty much on his own, though.

Learning Communication Skills from Dale Carnegie

""Tell me who your heroes are, and I"ll tell you who you"ll turn out to be."."

Upon returning from National Guard, he was determined to follow up on a long-ago vow to improve his public speaking. Warren was well aware that he was socially maladjusted and had to make amends if he wanted to succeed in life. He was also petrified by the thought of standing up on a stage and speaking to an audience; he felt queasy just by imagining such a scenario.

The stars seemed to be in perfect alignment because he soon mustered up the courage to finally enroll himself in Dale Carnegie's course on public speaking. Who else would have been a better teacher for Warren than a man whose strategies had been proven by data science?

He was happy to see that the people in the course were just like him: shy, reserved, and terrified with the thought of performing or speaking on the stage.

The course was based on numerous practical activities where Warren and his fellows had to read, memorize, and perform to present different excerpts. Gradually, with each other's support and the guidance of such an incredible mentor, Warren overcame his fear of public speaking. The skill assisted him in improving his salesmanship and helped him influence so many people today. Warren proudly refers to the course as "the most important degree" he possesses.

Warren could communicate with anyone now but failed miserably in talking to her crush Susie Thompson. The two had dated briefly in the summer before Columbia. Warren had tried wooing her since his return, but Susie always thought he was stuck up. Susie was much more mature than Warren, and instead of being fascinated by his prodigal mind, Susie thought he used it to show off or tear people down.

Hence, instead of directly pursuing Susie, Warren made good use of his smartness and came up with the idea to woo her father, Doctor Thompson. A psychologist himself, Doctor Thompson, understood from day one that Warren was going through all this trouble to impress him for the sake of his daughter. Though an intimidating man, he was always fatherly towards Warren and quite similar to Howard in many ways.

Warren was able to win Doctor Thompson over because of their similar religious and political beliefs. Both were protestants and supported Republicans. Susie was also dating a Jewish man at the time, which her father didn't approve of.

Warren used his tactics to convince Doctor Thompson, whose influence on his daughter was pretty evident. Susie had to go out with Warren on dates, but eventually, it turned out in her favor. Susie was quite bright as a journalism major, but she too had misunderstood Warren's socially weird behavior like others.

After spending some time with him, Susie saw Warren for who he indeed was beneath all that smart-aleck facade: an insecure boy who needs love and assurance. Warren was madly in love with her, and when Susie declared her love, Warren was quick to ask Doctor Thompson for Susie's hand in marriage. The two had an April wedding in 1952, and Warren Buffett now had his Mrs. Warren Buffett.

Him as an Investor: His Second Biggest Accomplishment

"In the world of business, the people who are most successful are those who are doing what they love."

Despite the surprising rejection from Graham-Newman, Warren was determined to earn money. So, he decided to do so by starting his own business. He wanted to deal in stocks but decided to leave New York for Omaha astonishingly. That was an odd decision as people dealing stocks considered Wall Street their Mecca, but Warren loved being close to people he valued.

Upon returning to Omaha, Warren was ready to venture out independently. However, he did need a second opinion and consulted the people he valued in this regard: Ben Graham, his mentor, and Howard Buffett, his father. To his surprise, both individuals advised Warren to wait for now instead of diving right into the messy world of stocks.

Warren valued their wisdom but knew this advice came from the fear the 1929 Great Depression had instilled in them and wanted Warren to play safe. Warren was an intelligent and stubborn individual who decided to go with his guts. His father supported him as he knew nothing could stand in Warren's way, who was a successful businessman since his teenage.

Warren decided to work for a firm while gaining some experience and knowledge regarding the operations of a stock business. He gave an interview at a local firm upon his father's request, but Warren had his eyes set on working at Buffett-Falk's firm. However, his duties did not include making calculations regarding the stocks, which he enjoyed, but selling stocks to customers instead.

Warren wasn't gifted in the department of interpersonal skills. He suffered as a salesman also due to his age; clients did not take Warren's predictions or advice seriously. They would be asking for his father's opinion instead. When Warren was nervous, he'd fire away all the information he had accumulated regarding a popular stock that people would then exploit and invest in; however, they would still not work with Warren. As a result, people made money, but Warren could not make commissions, the money upon which his job and livelihood depended.

Warren struggled at his job as a salesman and wanted to improve his public speaking skills. Therefore, he joined the University of Omaha as a teacher, following the steps of Graham. Warren used numerous analogies he had learned during his time as a student at Columbia, including the infamous Company A and Company B example. He wasn't the most patient teacher but gave out free advice regarding whatever company's name his students threw at him, just like Graham. He was also a strict teacher who didn't hand out favors or act biased.

Warren was soon going to have a family of three and knew he needed to make more money to provide for his family while fulfilling his dream of becoming a millionaire by 35. However, Warren had started losing money in his investments instead of earning more. These investments included buying shares of Cleveland Worsted Mill, a textile company, and buying a gas station opposite another gas station that had its loyal clientele running for decades. Warren also lost his friend's father's money, who never held a grudge against Warren, but Warren felt just as bad about losing other people's money as he felt for losing his own.

Warren, however, shifted this situation and started attracting clients through his reports on stocks and some through Graham's recommendations. Soon, he started managing people's money instead of just being a stockbroker. Graham's recommendation also landed him a job at American Securities, a well-known managing firm operated by the son of Sears CEO. Still, due to his duties as a National Guard, he couldn't go for it.

In 1954, Warren landed a job at Graham-Newman after countless struggles of making solid money and providing for his family. Luckily, the National Guard also allowed him to move this time as the job was in New York. He got the job because Graham had just lost his son and wasn't at his peak. Newman decided to get Warren on board. Soon Warren was able to charm everyone with his prodigal mind.

Warren lived frugally even now with his family. At the firm, he and Walter were busy looking for companies selling below the working capital. These companies are what Graham regarded as cigar butts. Graham had an eye for such companies.

Cigar butts were the almost dying companies that had some way of making money even after dying. The idea was to get one last puff or profit, in this case, from these companies before they liquidated their shares.

Though Graham was a champion at spotting such companies in Standard and Poor 500 and Moody's Manual, he didn't trust the volatile nature of business in these cases. Hence, he always tried to avoid such deals and bargains for himself. On the other hand, Warren started to get a hold of this investment approach and was soon practicing it for his stocks.

Warren made thousands of dollars through two deals in which he paid extra attention to the workings of the business: cocoa bean arbitrage and bus company stocks. The former was a deal where Graham had given up early in the game, but Warren decided to play it instead.

Just by holding onto the stocks for a longer time, Warren

made $13,000, whereas Graham had predicted $444 as

the best possible return. The latter made him $20,000.

Warren had soon started getting invites to the inner circle

parties at Newman's or sometimes at Graham's, thanks to

his brilliant mind making Graham-Newman some fortune.

However, in 1956, Graham decided to leave the

firm to enjoy his life instead of running wildly to make

money. Jerry Newman was also retiring, but his son

Mickey stayed and hoped Warren would take Graham's

place in the partnership. Warren was flattered by the

offer, but his goal was to learn under Graham's

mentorship. Besides, he knew Mickey would always have

the upper hand in the partnership, whereas Warren

preferred his partners to play a silent role. Hence, there

was no point in staying when his idol was leaving. His

career was also not going anywhere. He packed his bags

and returned to Omaha with a valuable experience to back

him in his career.

After returning to Omaha, Warren had initially planned on retiring. The compounding of his accumulated wealth would have made him a millionaire by 35, even if he had retired. However, his hunger to become a millionaire as early as possible did not let him sit idle, and Warren started planning a way to make money without a job. He wanted to work independently instead of taking orders from someone else; he wanted his genius to guide his decisions.

Hence, in 1956, he started Buffett Associates, Ltd., a hedge fund based on the model of Newman and Graham. Buffett had seven partners in this partnership: Warren's father-in-law Doc Thompson, Doris's husband, Truman Wood, Warren's aunt Alice Buffett, Warren's friend Chuck Peterson, Chuck Peterson's mother Elizabeth, Warren's lawyer Dan Monen, and Warren himself. He was determined to make these people he was close with heaps of money but wanted full autonomy with his investing decisions.

Warren also had numerous independent partnerships with people who were either relative with someone he knew or mostly Graham's connections and managed their money to make them profit. By the end of 1956, Warren had $4,500 in his earnings.

His lawyer and partner at Buffett's Associates, Dan Monen, withdrew his money from the partnership and brought forward another issue with which he needed Warren's help. Neither of them knew they would make thousands of dollars with this problem.

Dan had some bond certificates of National American Fire Insurance that weren't worth much because the business had started as a fraud. The company later began making profits, thanks to its changed management, but people were unaware of it. Instead of fighting for the certificates that Dan owned, Warren sent Dan on a mission to collect these certificates that the unscrupulous company initially sold to poor Nebraska farmers.

Dan went door-to-door paying small amounts for these certificates in the beginning. Innocent farmers were happy to get something out of the useless piece of paper. But soon, the word regarding the deal spread like wildfire, and Dan purchased the last of the certificate they could get his hands on for as high as a hundred bucks.

Soon Monen had collected two thousand shares that accounted for 10% of the company. Instead of transferring these shares in his name, Warren took the stocks and the original power of attorney to the company's head office and asked for the value transfer. Hence, just by Warren's habit of collecting, they had converted a piece of paper into real money.

Cigar Butt Investment Approach

"The investor of today does not profit from yesterday's growth."

Warren continued to make money for his partners on a much higher percentage than the market in total. He dealt in a low-risk, high-return way to beat the odds of losing money. His father's cancer diagnosis in 1958 made him even more driven to contribute to his business to avoid hearing its depressing details.

By 1959, thanks to the Davises, Warren was introduced to Charlie Munger, a successful lawyer, real estate investor, and businessman in Los Angeles with a much similar personality to Warren. The only difference was that Warren had his fair share of insecurities due to his prodigal mind, while Charlie took too much pride in his smartness. They understood each other differently than anybody else they had ever met.

Munger heard Buffett's accomplishments with fascination. However, unlike others drowning in awe or fearing the system due to its risk, Charlie wanted to start something similar in California. Soon, the two started spending their hard-earned dollars on phone bills and discussing new partners Charlie brought for Warren. The business was soon loosely expanding, but Warren was gaining support.

By 1961, Warren started his eleventh and the last partnership before dissolving it all in Buffett Private

Limited in 1962, whose 14 percent shares were owned by Warren's wife and daughter. Warren became a millionaire at thirty, but now he didn't want to stop. He was making thousands of dollars for his clients for an exuberant fee that people were willing to pay Warren, seeing him beat the market year by year.

Warren now knew that his home office wasn't going to be sufficient space for his ever-growing business logistically. He went on to buy a new workspace at Kiewit Plaza. He also hired his first-ever employee Bill Scott to manage Warren's files and calls.

Warren kept playing the old tricks he had mastered despite having a new office. However, despite the clean play, Warren suffered and barely made it out in some cases. One such case was dealing with Dempster Mill Manufacturing.

Dempster was a family business operated from Beatrice, Nebraska. In Warren's opinion, the town's windmills and irrigation system relied on the business that was dying out. The townspeople, however, didn't see it this way.

Warren became the chairman soon by buying out the company's stocks. However, the new manager kept buying new windmill parts left, right, and center, exhausting the company's cash. Warren knew he needed help and consulted Munger, who referred him to a man with skills in turning around businesses, Harry Bottle.

Harry started his work immediately, closing unwanted branches, selling unwanted inventory for a reasonable price, and bringing some money back to business. The company was now ready to be sold. However, to Warren's surprise, not many people were interested in the company.

To make matters worse, the townspeople of Beatrice raised funds to get rid of Buffett, a man they saw as an enemy because of the increase in turnover rate, bringing back the haunting memories of 1929. The people won against Buffett, who still made a profit, but he was scared from people's hatred, and the traumatic memory of this horrible incident through the cigar butt approach remains etched into his mind.

Meanwhile, Charlie Munger was on his way to steering away from the law and found his partnership with Jack Wheeler. The partnership was meant to run on Buffett private limited's business model. However, the difference between Warren's and Munger's approaches was the risk factor both were willing to take.

With mentors like his father and Graham, Warren had learned to become comfortable with playing it safe. Hence, cigar butts were his favorite type of business to invest in. Munger, however, liked to play it big thanks to his unwavering confidence in his abilities and genius. Munger dared Warren to try leaving his comfort zone, but Warren stayed firm on his approach.

Warren's safe and sound approach led him to flip Moody's Manual and find his cigar butts. Soon, he was looking at slightly bigger cigar butts and began investing. However, sometimes his track record of finding the best companies to liquidate and earn profit wasn't as squeaky clean. He went on to face one such company, but it led to the formation of what we call the Warren Buffett's Company Today.

Starting Berkshire Hathaway Inc.

"You only have to do a very few things right in your life so long as you don't do too many things wrong."

Warren went on to play in the fields of Massachusetts this time. He found a textile mill named Berkshire Hathaway. The American textile industry was failing then, and most companies were folding their companies and factories. Warren went for Berkshire Hathaway with the same intention but was soon proved wrong.

Seabury Stanton, the president of Berkshire Hathaway, was a man of vision. However, his vision was limited. It had him focused only on saving Hathaway in any way possible due to its sentimental value as a family business. A hurricane in 1954 ruined every single project of the Hathaway plant. Instead of closing down the company, he merged it with Berkshire Fine Mill. But both the companies, now incorporated into Berkshire Hathaway, couldn't keep themselves afloat.

Stanton, however, wasn't looking to lose hope anytime soon. He was determined to save his life's hard work. That determination and stubbornness in trying to keep a failing business became a hurdle for Buffett.

Buffett invested his partnership money into various companies, including American Express, which had a significant case against them after JFK's assassination. Warren had testified against them because his father's ethics and principles slowly surfaced in him. Warren then went on to invest in Berkshire Hathaway in 1962. According to his firm's calculation, Berkshire Hathaway was worth $19.46 per share, but the stocks were still selling at the price of peanuts for less than ten bucks.

Warren started buying stocks through his partners as he knew that if his name got associated with the stocks, they would raise the price. He told two of his partners to keep buying because he knew Seabury would come forward to buy it from them at whatever price he asked. The time came soon but brought with it something that Warren wasn't prepared for, and in retrospect, neither was Seabury.

Warren met Seabury to negotiate the prices of the stocks of Berkshire Hathaway, at which Warren would sell it to Seabury. They decided on a price that made Warren a couple of bucks per share. When Warren went home, he saw another deal people were talking about in papers regarding the stocks of Berkshire Hathaway: Seabury was offering an even higher price to whoever wanted to sell the company's stocks.

Seabury's trick infuriated Warren, and he set out one of his partners under whose name he was buying the stocks to talk to Seabury and stop the deal. To make matters worse, Seabury refused to make any deal between them entirely. The two of them argued, but soon Seabury had to pay as Warren was now determined to buy out the whole company.

Instead of selling, he was now buying stocks of Berkshire Hathaway. He set out his people to buy enough stocks to get him on the board, and that's what happened. Due to the sudden popularity and Buffett's interest in the firm, some of his friends also set out to enjoy the coattail ride, but Warren bought them out as they could see how vital every stock was to Warren. And who'd ever decide to go against him?

Warren also arranged a meeting to understand Berkshire's operations as Buffett always does to understand the business. Though he had planned to meet Jack Stanton, Seabury's son and successor, Jack sent for Ken Chace due to his busy schedule. That turned out to be a perfect situation as Otis, Seabury's brother and a significant share owner, never thought Jack was fit for the part and had an interest in making Ken Chace the president.

Ken Chace, vice president of manufacturing, patiently took Buffett on a two-day tour around the factory. He answered and elaborated on every query Buffett had. He proved to be a man of value, and Buffett had his eyes set on him since that day to give him a director's position once Buffett owned the company.

To own a significant percentage of Berkshire Hathaway, Buffett met and wooed Otis Stanton. Though a family business, Otis never enjoyed the sight of his brother driving the company into heaps of destruction by making one wrong decision after another. Otis readily agreed to sell all of his two thousand shares to Buffett, hoping something good would finally come out of this investment and turn around the fate of the dooming business Berkshire Hathaway.

With the majority of shares and majority support from the board of Berkshire, Warren succeeded in getting elected as the chairman of the company in 1965. He then appointed Ken Chace as the president and gave all the responsibility of running operations to the much deserving, talented, and dedicated man. The board also saw some fake weeping and disappointing show of resignation from the former president Seabury and his son Jack but were finally happy to get rid of them.

The local newspaper was interested in the story and started calling Buffett an outsider. Since Dempster's miserable happenings were forever etched on Warren's memory, he set out to publicly change the narrative around this time. He went on to erase his image as a liquidator. He told the media that he was interested in keeping the business running, and there'd be no folding or closing of mills in the area regarding Berkshire Hathaway. The public promise he made Warren now had to keep.

Cigar butts were the only way Buffett ever knew to make incredible profits for his partners. But during that era, with nuclear war as a threat, he had seen a shift in the market. He now had millions of dollars to invest but not enough cigar butts to invest in.

This situation and lack of opportunities made him worried about how he would manage so many partners that depended upon him. The last people he added to his partnership were his children. He sold the Nebraska farm he owned and used the price to buy shares of Berkshire Hathaway as an investment for his children and to raise his stakes in the company.

Buffett now had to look at bigger businesses to run if he genuinely wanted to make dollars for his partners. Though not his specialty, Buffett paid attention to his much-regretted investment Berkshire Hathaway. He wanted to send out a clear message to his spectators that he didn't plan to leave the business hanging by a thread nor look forward to liquidating it. However, Warren knew he had to do something to solve his problems in investing.

Soon Warren was trying to meet his commitment and working tirelessly to keep Berkshire Hathaway running. The textile was not part of Buffett's circle of competence. Hence, he had started regretting the deal as soon as he had made it.

He got a trusted auditor Verne McKenzie at New Bedford, to look after the doomed textile mill. Buffett had made some impossible decisions of getting the distribution running at a low cost, something he would have never done earlier in the day. He had also started selling the company's shares to get more people, ideas, and money into the business.

However, once he realized that more shareholders didn't mean more honest and loyal shareholders, he offered an excellent price for the shares of Berkshire Hathaway. Those who took the dividend being provided on the shares by Buffett left the company, and he knew they weren't the people who cared about the business.

In contrast, the shareholders who stayed had some liking towards the business and would have brought some of their visions to the sinking business. That's how Warren narrowed down the circle of people working on Berkshire while ensuring the quality of the business.

Warren had started learning numerous things about the textile mill and the textile business in general. He wanted to understand how the business worked to think more about the ideas of making it resurface from its doom. Textile, in general, was a failing industry in America, where the entire nation was already facing issues of layoffs, causing unemployment.

Warren listened earnestly to Chace and McKenzie. They had managed to close several divisions that weren't making a profit. However, all of them soon realized that closing divisions weren't the solution as the problem with Berkshire was quite different. Berkshire Hathaway required more investment in large areas, including machinery.

If Warren had gone with that decision, he would have just seemed like another Seabury, watering a desert in futile hopes of keeping a business going. Warren was scared of the Dempster incident repeating itself. Therefore, he had to soon come up with a way to keep people at their jobs while not investing loads of money in a business that would never pay profits in return.

Since Warren also had his partnership business to look after, he also had to make up for the hasty decision of Berkshire. He sold many American Express shares the partnership owned for a reasonable price. But he was now stuck deciding where to put the money; he knew his partners didn't deserve their money reinvesting in Berkshire. It was a lost cause.

Warren had his eyes set on another business in Omaha. National Indemnity was an insurance company run by a man named Jack Ringwalt. The man's vision and ideas quite inspired Warren as he had started by ensuring the most trivial things and random people who didn't otherwise think of insuring themselves, such as circus entertainers, etc.

It was tough to get his hands on National Indemnity, though. Ringwalt had only one episode every year during which he'd want to sell the company. Warren was just waiting for that one golden chance. He had his friend working at National Indemnity on alert so that Warren could grab the opportunity whenever Ringwalt decided to sell. And that's what he did.

In February of 1967, there came a day when Ringwalt decided to sell his business. Charlie Heider, Warren's friend and a board member of National Indemnity, communicated this news to Warren immediately, who didn't waste a second in arranging the meeting for the very same day.

As soon as Buffett and Ringwalt met, Buffett instantly agreed to all that Ringwalt was offering without even the slightest change. He understood the volatile nature of the deal and didn't want to jeopardize it with his stubbornness.

Ringwalt immediately regretted selling the business he had started and sustained with his hard work. But a man of his words, Ringwalt didn't back out from the deal. However, he invested the money he had earned from the deal in Berkshire Hathaway.

The Secret Behind Warren Buffett's Success

Invest in What You Love

"In the world of business, the people who are most successful are those who are doing what they love."

Let Go of History

"If past history was all that is needed to play the game of money, the richest people would be librarians."

Warren had seen brilliant minds like his mentor Graham and his father drowned still in mourning 1929's Great Depression. Both had great potential but opted to play safe instead. Warren was never a believer in playing it safe, nor was he the one to hold onto history.

One can only learn so much from history. However, the world is changing, and the marketplace is constantly evolving with new ideas and ventures. A technological revolution is underway. So, there's not much to look at history for. Looking back only messes with your neck.

Warren believes in looking ahead and charging at the future with all your might and genius. He loved taking calculated risks and did so no matter what the history said. He believed in math and the pattern more than in the past and learned to deal with his investments instead of logically.

You should never hold back when pursuing something, especially if that's the goal you've been meaning to achieve for ages. Never hold yourself in history. There's a reason it's gone.

Being stuck in history will never let you move forward. Life lies in the today, and investments made today give returns in the future. There's no role of history in the investment world.

Understand Then Invest

"Buy a stock the way you would buy a house. Understand and like it such that you'd be content to own it in the absence of any market."

Buffett is often asked in interviews regarding his decision not to invest in Microsoft or Amazon. He replies that these companies run a business out of his circle of competence. It means that he's unable to understand the future of these companies as such companies in technology and the internet are consistently revolutionizing themselves.

Warren has always advised us to invest in the things that we understand. Taking calculated risks is always important, which requires first comprehending the calculations or, in other words, the business's operations.

Making informed choices is crucial to avoid losing money, which Warren has never personally enjoyed. That's also the most significant reason he hasn't invested in cryptocurrency, a new marketplace that's making people millionaires overnight, but Warren can't understand its notion and doesn't play with it.

Therefore, investing in businesses and companies that interest you or that you understand is crucial. Not everyone is gifted to understand the workings of big pharma, but some are excellently talented at it. Others might be knowledgeable and even interested in dealing with real estate businesses. Whatever the industry, understand then invest.

Purchase When Price Falls

"Most people get interested in stocks when everyone else is. The time to get interested is when no one else is. You can't buy what is popular and do well."

While people tend to sell when the market crashes or the price falls, a good investor must buy. That's the perfect time for investment as you can get your hands on stocks for a bargain price. If the market is doing well, the prices are high; there is no room for buying much.

When everybody wants a share, the prices go high. When people don't want the shares, they sell, and the prices crash. Sometimes dying companies are worth more than the living, which Buffett practiced in his early days.

Warren had made a good investment from the shares his mentor Ben Graham wanted to sell. Buying low and earning high returns on a company's shares when it's under the process of liquidation is the cigar butt approach that Warren has now stopped but earned commendable profits from.

Hence, when investing, look for calculated risks but buy at low costs. You can buy many cheap stocks, which would ultimately result in a rise in price if the company is not folding. Holding onto those shares for a while or forever, if possible, is your way to earn high profits.

Make Fear a Friend

"Widespread fear is your friend as an investor because it serves up bargain purchases."

Let history prove that the market has always risen back up even from the worst crashes. Whether it was the postwar Great Depression or the faulty insurance policies leading to the Recession, businesses have gotten back on their feet, and people have persevered to regain their glory.

Still, these times are considered the worst times for people as they lead their lives in fear, but for an investor, such times are golden.

When the market has gone haywire, and more than logic, people follow fear and sell away their stocks, a good investor always buys them instead of folding. As the market survives the times, the stock prices will skyrocket, and that's when investors make money. Hence, fear should be your best friend in the world of investments.

Warren had seen this pattern of fear in people post the Great Depression, which kept others from taking risks, but he managed to earn profits even from the dying businesses; his cigar butt approach is notoriously famous for making him thousands of dollars.

Invest in Yourself

"The most important investment you can make is in yourself."

Warren has always been a firm believer in investing in yourself. He has followed this advice by being an avid reader from an early age, reading all the books in his father's library, and going to businesses in person and asking them questions to understand their operations better.

Warren believed that investing in yourself will get you the highest return on investment. Therefore, he chose to enroll in Columbia to learn from his heroes, David Dodd and Benjamin Graham, two of the most resonating names in the world of investment.

Warren also highly revered his Dale Carnegie Public Speaking degree that he has framed and up on his office wall. That degree gradually aided him in becoming a teacher and a good salesman.

Investing in yourself is crucial. You can learn from online resources, get certifications, or learn self-sufficiently through reading books. To make informed choices, one must be informed first. No investment other than education can help you stay ahead and avoid losses.

Keep yourself updated on the latest market trends, read newspapers, and seek mentors with the expertise you desire. Spend on educating yourself. Never limit yourself when it comes to learning something.

Be Patient

"Our favorite holding period is forever."

Warren learned his lesson on patience early with his first-ever stock investment. He had bought Cities Service Preferred shares at $38 and sold them in a few months for $40 as the prices had initially dropped.

However, after selling the stocks, the prices spiked to $202.

The first-ever stock experiment had introduced him to the golden nugget of patience that Warren held onto with his dear life. He was then able to make large sums of profits throughout his career just by holding onto a company's stocks for months, if not years. That's how he had made Dan Monen huge sums with bond certificates.

Hence, patience is crucial for making big in the world of investment. If you're looking for a get-rich scheme, know that you won't find much return. However, if you can hold those stocks for a decade or two or even forever that you've wisely invested in a company, stocks can build you a fortune. For investing in stocks, be patient; for everything else in life, be relentless until you achieve it.

Look for Fair Price, Not Fair Company

"It's far better to buy a wonderful company at a fair price than a fair company at a wonderful price."

Because of his cigar butt investments, Warren had made a lot of money, but he had also lost a lot of his precious time that, in retrospect, he thinks he could have invested in other ventures. For him, Berkshire Hathaway, the holding company he owns, was his worst investment because the cigar butt was a fair price but not a fair company. He learned the same lesson from investing in Dempster and realized that cigar butts aren't worth the hassle.

Charlie Munger, Warren's partner and advisor, also pushed Warren to look for businesses that would stay in the long run, no matter their price. Investing in a company whose values and operations speak for themselves is a good move, even if its stock price is higher than the cigar butts. Companies with fair business dealings and vision are likely to make more money than those prone to dying.

When looking for investments, Warren prohibits following his old habits of buying cigar butts. He explains a cigar butt as a soggy cigar with one last puff remaining. That one last profit is certainly not worth the troubles that come with it, such as the business eating up your money or the reputation it costs.

If you're investing in a business, take a calculated risk but never with a cigar butt. Look for a good company whose current operations and future projections are evident and understandable, and the business is of some interest to you.

In today's era, making such a choice isn't so tough as numerous businesses are seen soaring in the world of technology, and the future holds many more opportunities. Just remember Warren's advice and know when the iron is hot to strike for a price the company is worth, even if higher than a cheap cigar butt.

Invest, Invest, INVEST

"Today, people who hold cash equivalents feel comfortable. They shouldn't. They have opted for a terrible long-term asset, one that pays virtually nothing and is certain to depreciate in value."

From an early age, Warren had understood the power of compounding and trained his mind to look for new ways of generating income using his money. These early ideas and ventures contributed to Warren's success as they made him seek ways of making money work for him. He also understood that keeping money saved over time will only give us the same money back but for a decrease in value.

Warren has never been in favor of keeping money stored in a bank. Banks use people's money and provide it as a loan with a higher interest to others desperately in need. In short, banks make our money work for them. How does that provide value to us?

Warren has therefore emphasized numerous times that money loses its value over the years due to the increase in the rate of inflation. Hence, people need to invest money to earn a profit of some percentage.

He suggests buying stocks of a business that we understand to grasp how the company operates. This way, we would be able to predict the market at times and sell

stocks to earn a profit. However, Warren also suggests
holding onto the stocks for the most extended period as
the stocks would grow in value over the years, especially if
the business we invest in belongs to an ever-growing
industry.

It's essential to take risks and invest. Saving will get
us nowhere with money, as money is just some bills and
coins that would depreciate in value over the years. We
might be able to buy candy for a dollar, but perhaps in the
next few years, the price of the candy might rise, and then
that dollar saved for buying a candy won't be enough.

Hence, no matter what you do, educate yourself
regarding investing, gain information about the businesses
you are interested in and then invest your capital and hold
onto it for as long as possible.

Invest, earn a profit, and then invest that profit to
make more profit. Never save money.

Becoming successful doesn't require paying
exuberant amounts for luxury goods or dressing in

branded clothes. Hence, one can minimize expenses by turning that money into a high-paying investment to be successful and wealthy. Being rich is an easy task; buy all the lottery tickets sold, and one would make you rich. Sustainability makes you wealthy and financially independent in the longer run.

A Penny Saved Is a Penny Earned

"Predicting rain doesn't count; building the ark does."

David Dodd, Warren's cherished mentor, was the one to coin the phrase "a penny saved is a penny earned." Though no one might have paid heed to it, Warren took it to his heart. Therefore, he understood the value of money and is still well-known for his frugal living habits.

Despite being a billionaire, he lives in his 1958 bought house, eats McDonald's meals daily, and drives an old car. Unlike some of today's millionaires, he neither has a flashy lifestyle nor a large villa to show off. He is the same as he was back in his early days when he dressed in old clothes and lived at the YMCA. Warren always lands himself the cheapest deals on something as trivial as old newspaper collections.

Give Back

"If you're in the luckiest 1% of humanity, you owe it to the rest of humanity to think about the other 99%."

Susie Buffett was giving by nature. She had a motherly affection towards everyone she met, including Warren. Her nurturing attention made her a big name in philanthropy that Warren continued to keep even after her death.

Susie had donated to numerous charities in the name of her father-in-law Howard Buffett. She and Warren had contributed to the goal of quality education for as many young students as possible. She also worked tirelessly to make Warren aware of his share of responsibilities towards society.

Buffett lowered his win percentage against the market during the time of Dr. King's movement for this reason. He wanted to make more time for the community and help the people of Omaha fight against segregation.

Instead of just keeping his focus on the black community's rights, Warren also stood up for the Jewish community, another marginalized group in Omaha at that time. He understood, opened his eyes to the privileges he enjoyed, and spoke in favor of equality in all stances.

After Susie died in 2012, Warren also started the Giving Pledge movement. In this pledge, he has promised to give away 90% of the wealth he has accumulated over the years. He also invited other billionaires to contribute to this noble cause and has been supported by big names in the tech industry, such as Bill Gates and Mark Zuckerberg.

Warren contributes majorly to the Bill and Melinda Gates Foundation, which work primarily toward quality education and award scholarships to students worldwide on a merit basis. He also donates money to his children's charities and helps the less privileged.

Despite his unempathetic and immature nature during his early life, Warren grew up to be a man who understood his role in society. He lives frugally and has enough wealth to feed himself and others. And so, he chooses to give back to the community.

This piece of advice is crucial to remember. By giving back to the world through wealth, time or knowledge, we're only making this world a better place. If the rich only learn how to receive and never give, the unbalanced population economically will soon prove to be detrimental to society in general.

Learn to give whatever you can to leave this world a better place.

Read Daily

"Read 500 pages like this every day. That's how knowledge works. It builds up like compound interest. All of you can do it, but I guarantee not many of you will do it."

Warren had started reading about investing at the age of seven. That's how he came up with ideas for making investments in small businesses. Later in life, Ben Graham and David Dodd's bestselling book in the field of investing, The Intelligent Investor, changed Buffett's life at 19.

Imagine if all of that wouldn't have happened for Buffett? He probably would have never gone to Columbia, learned a great deal about the rules of investing that have made him an incredible and the most famous investor of all time, and we probably won't have been learning from him. Warren has accumulated all the wealth over the years because of Warren's love for reading.

While other kids his age back in the days were busy playing outdoor sports, Warren was found at a library with his head in the book. He had books like Moody's Manual at his disposal, from which he later got ideas for his cigar butt investments. Warren might have been just an ordinary child if he hadn't been into reading since an early age.

Even today, though not as fast as in his youth, Warren reads for 5 to 6 hours daily. He reads at least five daily newspapers to keep himself updated with the current happenings of the world and the investment business. He often finds new ideas for investment from papers that keep his business growing forever.

Reading is a simple task. Anyone can do it because it's easy, and books and newspapers aren't hard to get in today's era of technology. The real question is will we take Warren's no-cost advice to keep ourselves knowledgeable and well-informed to make good decisions? You might already be on the staircase to success if you've read so far.

Be Inspired, Not Influenced

"I had a great teacher in life, my father. But I had another great teacher in terms of profession in Ben Graham. I was lucky enough to get the right foundation very early on. And then, basically, I didn't listen to anybody else. I look in the mirror every morning, and the mirror always agrees with me. And I go out and do what I believe I should be doing. And I'm not influenced by what other people think."

Warren was fascinated with Ben Graham. Graham's ideas and recommendations that he freely gave to whoever asked were respected back in the day. But there were many things that both didn't agree on.

The cigar butt approach, for instance, was never worth much for Graham, but Warren understood the process and made thousands from it. Similarly, when Graham suggested Warren should hold off jumping into the investment business world, Warren respected it but didn't go with it. These examples show that Warren was inspired by his mentors, not influenced by them.

The Great Depression had left great minds like his mentor Graham and his father Howard Buffett playing it safe in the world. But they were also not interested in money itself as Warren was. Hence, Warren always looked to them for strength and support but always went with his genius mind and abilities to calculate precisely before making a big decision.

The same is the case between Buffett and Munger. The two usually think alike, but Warren always finds a way to get around him for the investments he believes in if the two disagree.

Hence, being inspired and being influenced are two separate things. You can have idols and still choose a different path than them. The goal is to be a person of your own instead of a second-hand version of an already well-known personality.

Nobody knows Warren today for Ben Graham: people know Warren for his accomplishments. You'll never be able to accomplish anything if you're trying to become influenced by them and turn into a miniature of your idols. Learn to pave your own path.

Time Is Money

"You've gotta keep control of your time, and you can't unless you say no. You can't let people set your agenda in life."

In many interviews, Warren refers to Berkshire Hathaway as his worst mistake. Although the business turned out in his favor, he still regrets the time and effort he wasted on turning Berkshire into a successful business. According to Warren, he could have spent that time building another company from scratch that would have generated even more profit for him than Berkshire.

In the world of investment, time is money. Although the phrase is coined on various occasions, it is practically true for investments. A day's delay can cause you to lose a fair-priced stock, or just a day earlier in selling a stock can cost you money, as it did to Warren when he bought Cities Services Preferred.

Warren has always taken calculated risks with a good margin of safety. He has never made any bets that would be against this principle. But with calculated risks, he also calculated the time to take those risks. Since time is money, one can play the cards early but never late.

When investing or dealing with important decision-making, always ensure that you're on time; making delayed decisions might serve you no good as the market fluctuates hourly. Many of the investments and trading depend on political affairs. Hence, if you're looking for a perfect deal, ensure you're pursuing it at the perfect time.

Dream and Believe

"I always knew I was going to be rich. I don't think I ever doubted it for a minute."

Warren had first decided to start his own business right out of Columbia. However, two of the most significant people in his life, Ben Graham, Warren's mentor, and Howard Buffett, Warren's father, asked him to wait.

They thought it was perhaps not the right time for the young and eager Warren, who still needed to mature. However, Warren had no doubts about being successful. So, he decided to go with his heart and believe in himself. That's how we know his many great adventures and risks in the world of investments today.

He went on to manage people's money, start partnerships and hedge funds, and turn a dying textile business nobody knew of into a profitable venture that people still trust. Could Warren have these achievements if he had waited for the right time even when his gut told him otherwise? No. That's the power of belief!

He dreamed of becoming a millionaire by 35 at 15, and he never doubted himself throughout his journey. He saw a dream, chased it day and night, and never looked back.

Warren's resilience helped him stand out from the crowd of entrepreneurs. His relentless approach and constant thoughts about growing his wealth led him to become a millionaire and then a billionaire. This dedication and steadfastness got him to this stage.

If you're pursuing something, go at it with full force. Believe in yourself that you will be successful. So, instead of taking no and retrieving disheartened, you must relentlessly pursue what you believe in your heart is for you.

What one's mind can imagine, one can achieve.

Conclusion

Warren was a bright kid since his childhood. People who knew him closely often proclaimed him a prodigy. His love for reading and aptitude for numbers made him start his journey into the world of business and investing early in the day. However, his passion and interest in making money have made him a big shot today.

Warren may have had self-esteem issues that he compensated for with his sharp-mindedness, but he was always sure that he would become a millionaire. And even after becoming one, he didn't stop; he kept updating his goals as complacency is the downhill ride for businesses.

Warren's story isn't extraordinary, but his attention to detail and taking the initiative at the right time make him unbeatable. He loves making money but isn't greedy in this regard and values fair and ethical business strategies because his father's principles are far too intricately woven into his personality to show otherwise. Warren's story makes us believe that we, too, can succeed, but there are certain things we must do to achieve this.

Warren is a man who relentlessly pursues his goals without shame or wasting a minute considering other people's opinions. His efforts were extraordinary, but the actions are doable. You, too, can take Warren's advice shared in this book and make a fortune for yourself. The market may seem too competitive in today's era, with start-ups on every corner. Still, with the will, determination, and proper research and information, you can make informed decisions and succeed.

Disclaimer